Eating Pears on the Rooftop

poems by

David Estringl

Finishing Line Press
Georgetown, Kentucky

Eating Pears
on the Rooftop

Copyright © 2022 by David Estringel
ISBN 978-1-64662-921-3 First Edition
All rights reserved under International and Pan-American Copyright Conventions. No part of this book may be reproduced in any manner whatsoever without written permission from the publisher, except in the case of brief quotations embodied in critical articles and reviews.

ACKNOWLEDGMENTS

Many thanks to the wonderful mentors and publications that have supported my work and me over the years…

Mef Hardin
Terror House Magazine
Former People Journal
Salt Ink
Writ in Dust
Cajun Mutt Press
littledeathlit
Expat Press
Foliate Oak Magazine
Cephalopress
Setu Bilingual Journal
The Bitchin' Kitsch
45 Magazine
Alien Buddha Press

Publisher: Leah Huete de Maines
Editor: Christen Kincaid
Cover Art: ChooStudio
Author Photo: David Estringel

Order online: www.finishinglinepress.com
also available on amazon.com

Author inquiries and mail orders:
Finishing Line Press
PO Box 1626
Georgetown, Kentucky 40324
USA

Table of Contents

Kiss Me, Again, Again, and Again 1

Lithium 2

Blue Room 3

Gin & Tonic on a Sunday Afternoon 4

Sucking the Marrow 5

Coffeehouse Romance 6

And the Beat Goes On 8

Old Filament, Broken Bulb 10

Blue Sky through Bare Branches 11

Storms 12

Killers 14

Smooth Whiskey 15

Just Another Day 16

joshua 17

life in/verse 18

Burn 19

Digging for Lost Temples 21

Cajeta (Gimme Some Sweet!) 23

Coda-Switch 25

little deaths 27

Duende 29

Eating Pears on the Rooftop 30

Kiss Me, Again, Again, and Again

The coppery taste of meat beneath your sweet breath lingers
like a penny on the tip of my tongue.
Heads or tails?
Can't lose—
Lucky me.
My equilibrium's fucked raw,
as my hands drink-in the warm curvature of your hips.
O, glorious spit—
a little dab will do ya—
streaked red and hot,
never take me from this place,
leaving me
haunted by the ghost of that breath—
your Heaven,
your Hell—
that leaves me…
quivering.
Words can't capture what's smeared on this cheek
by fingers,
sticky and sweet—
so why try.
Kiss me,
again,
again,
and again,
in that white muslin dress of thigh-stretched daisies
that roll and grin like morning shadows,
smiling at secrets hidden in dark places.

Lithium

Dishes are piled high in the sink.
Papers strewn about
(My business for none to see).
Cobwebs frame doorways,
waving, familiarly, in silent clamor.
I walk these floors,
dirt beneath bare feet
from many roads taken
and the soles of passersby.
Stumbling,
I pass books stacked high on chairs and tabletops.
(No more room on the shelves)
Ones I'll always remember. Ones I chose to forget. Ones never to be read.
How funny it is to see this place
(This place where I live, rosy-hued),
when the switch is flicked.
God, this place needs a good cleaning!

Blue Room

Nights are hardest to bear,
alone, atop these unwashed sheets
that smell of you and me, still,
crinkled and heavy with ghosts
of our sweat and loving juices.
I am tethered
to flashes of smiles and kisses
that linger beneath the sweetness of heated exhales.
To smell your breath, again,
and taste you on the back of my tongue.
To pull you into me by the small of your back
and sink into the warmth of white musk—
a tangle of tongues, fingers, and limbs.
To have you, know you, again,
inside and out, is all I want.
Need.
Laying here, drowning in us,
my legs brush against the cold rustle of sheets you left behind,
cutting the airlessness of this room.
Rolling over, I close my eyes
and sink my face into the depths of your pillow,
escaping the void that even silence's ring has forgotten,
and take you in, drowning in us,
this lover's kaddish.
The scent of your hair—
blue fig and orange—and spit,
 are but pebbles on the gravestone.

Gin & Tonic on a Sunday Afternoon

Bitter on the lips,
spirits of juniper berries bless and honey tongues
with bite and fire.
Sugared words
that have long abandoned us
take wing in ambrosial flight from our dark corners—
winter suns—
thawing the frost that hardens our hearts
and tender fingertips.
Chestnut hair falls before your eyes,
as you read, biting your lip—
the smell of you, tearing
like a machete
through bands of cigarette smoke that haunt the air between us.
You go to the kitchen to make us another drink.
Suckin' gin from ice cubes,
I sit,
worshiping you—silently, in reverie—for letting me miss you,
again.
But that's the story of you and I—
hard to swallow save these fleeting moments—
like bubbles at the back of the throat that make us smile.
Looking out the window,
clouds drifting across pale azure,
I wonder where the Hell I've been all this time,
as crickets join in the fun—
even if just for a while.

Sucking the Marrow

Crackling
of hungry drags
from flaming cigarette cherries.
Tinkling
of ice cubes
from sweaty glasses,
thirsty
for heavy splashes of gin.
Ringing
from the silence
of words
that have had their due.
Waiting…
Waiting…
Waiting…
Crackling.
Tinkling.
Ringing.
Waiting…
Waiting…
Waiting…
for the soothing balm
of
"I'm leaving."

Coffeehouse Romance

I see you,
alone,
reading Raymond Carver
at a table for two.
Straight, black hair—
lightly greased—
falling in your face.
You brush it away,
saving a page
with your right thumb,
I notice
the smoothness
of your hands,
the fullness
of your fingers.
Your eyes
are lost in ugly life—
I think they are brown.
The angles
and curves
of your face
sing
in silent poetry.
You turn a page.
I long
to dip my face
into your cupped hands
and drink in
the smell of you.
To taste the sweat of your palms.
To kiss the fingertips
that have touched
the sum of your parts.

You catch my eye,
so I look away.
You keep reading.
I wonder—
for a moment—
what it's like
to be that chair.
You close your book
and get up to leave.
Passing me by—
warm—
smelling
of faded cologne
and sweaty jeans,
I devour you
at every inhale.
You leave me,
unaware
that for a moment
you
were everything
that mattered—
my *Cathedral*—
and with the ghosts of fingerprints
lingering upon my tongue.

And the Beat Goes On

Dropping from the air
upon ears like paper blotters on willing tongues,
raging at the bloodlessness of cardboard cutouts against a shrinking sky,
through psychedelic lenses
let me seeeee, let me beeeee the pulse of silent rage
that rails against the vulgar machine
with words
that organize, legitimize, minimize, super-size, tranquilize,
proselytize, tantalize, infantilize,
sexualize, stigmatize the suckled teats of long-conditioned truths.

Poking the bear, disturbing the seas of featureless beige,
stirring the comatose anima with battle-cries of sight and sound
that pierce dusty eardrums like sterling icepicks,
repressed wants teeeeem, solemn faces beeeeeam,
liberated in the warmth of a sun that breaks just beyond the horizon
on coffee-house stages,
rousing thoughts
to gestate, ruminate, conjugate, propriate, sublimate, fornicate,
obliterate, determinate,
propagate, exfoliate dangerous visions, birthed from the
unfetteredness of a purple haze.

Fueling the scribblings of furious hands upon white sheets with
whisky and cigarettes,
Making, naked, ugly underbellies of the angst-ridden and inflamed
with the glorious promises of their ecstatic treasure-trails,
let's revel in the coolness of poetry's heeeeeat, indulged in pollen-dusted skin so sweeeeet
within the honeyed tangles of poets' asymmetries
to detoxify, dulcify, intensify, demystify, purify, glorify, magnify,
beautify, electrify, sanctify
our bodily streams of light that sugar lips and candy the fingertips.

Tearing away at the fabric, unraveling, woven from Gloopstick youth and plasticine smiles,
repulsing at the hoards in their mindless quests for extra-flavor and double-coupon days,
looking for a steeeeeal, wanting to feeeeel,
as hollow dollars crumble to coins when plopped upon unsated palms and countertops.
Think! Think! Think! Think! Think!
We are on the brink
of the Fall of the American Empire.

Dig.

Old Filament, Broken Bulb

A white bolt from above
rips
through the clouds before our eyes—
an epiphany—
showering cuts upon the kitchen table,
releasing bad blood,
testing our guile
and gristle.

Blue Sky through Bare Branches

I look, upwards, at blue sky through bare branches,
the dewy wet of cool, green grass on my back,
clinging,
sinking,
pulling me further away from this place.
I long for the stillness of being
found only in the shedding of this meat that plants me here.
Oh, to touch those spaces in-between.
To graze my lips upon that azure skin.
O, opiate kiss,
like a stone, skipping across limpid pools,
let me caress that face with my lips and sink into your oblivion.
Your everything!
But I am bound,
here,
by bare branches,
between me and a beckoning sky.
Biting my lip to taste blood,
I long to smear red what God has painted blue.

Storms

We live for moments like this,
you and I,
cooled by the safe-silence
of deadened air—
a stillness so heavy
it falls,
crashing around our feet
with the tumult
of resting heartbeats.
I can think.
You can breathe.
We can just…be
for a moment,
until…

But nothing lasts forever
in the eye.
Tears—like rain—must fall,
staining, tattering
cheeks and lips,
eroding the ground
beneath us,
where we stand.
And that deadly call
within me
like the wind
must howl,
breaking the chain of calm
that threatens
to drown
me
in the deep
of my own waters.

Nothing
can save us.
Not you.
Not me.
Not all the friends in the world.
I am lost
without the thunder.
Without the swell
and crashing of waves—
the murk
that lies
beneath this skin.
Quiet slips away
and I
howl…
driving you,
lovingly,
to warm shelter
away
from me
and my storms.
Just remember me, fondly,
dear friend…when it rains.

Killers

I cut you
with words
to watch you bleed.
You starve me
with silence
to see me wither.
Funny,
we should look back
upon that lifeless heap
we left—
surprised—
each wondering,
"How could you let that happen?"

Smooth Whiskey

tick…tock
tick…tock
The days are long in a life of slow motion. Waking up takes too long, despite the violent assaults of the alarm clock, unchained by a snooze button—like me—worn down to the circuitry.
tick…tock
tick…tock
Get up late, again. Take a whore bath in the bathroom sink. Wash what needs it and get out the door. Shower'd be nice…really nice. Maybe tomorrow. Probably not…again.
tick…tock
tick…tock
Office clocks—harbingers of death to my soul—lament the dying of the fire, within. Telephone rings perforate the recirculated air of lungs and mouths like a symphony of electric crickets, tuning-up beneath the hepatic glow of fluorescent suns outside my cubicle's walls.
tick…tock
tick…tock
Driving home in the same car, down the same roads, in the same rancid clothes that need more than just a good airing out, stuck in this bad track mix, playing on a loop, I need a drink. There's a bottle at home. Whiskey, I think—a gift for my 50th. It goes down, rough, but smooth, after a glass or two or three.
Smooth is good in a life of no motion.
tick…tock
tick…tock

(Repeat All)

Just Another Day

It's been a week since you left
and tore a hole in my atmosphere,
letting in the gamma rays,
the end of days:
all in a haze
of tears and holographic "I'm sorries."

Was it you?
Was it me
that left everything
broken?
For a new love to find?
To be cruel to be kind?
Escaping a bind
that catches the skin like fingers of crushed glass.

I find myself,
standing outside the home we made,
wishing these arms—those walls—
could hold you, again.
A chance to feel—
a moment to steal—
but our fate is sealed
with all being said
and done.

If only
I could evaporate
up
into the clouds
of that noon sky and rain down
somewhere—
anywhere—
without a care
far…
far…
away…
from here.

joshua

I heard, today, that you died nine years ago.
My friend wasn't sure—said he heard whispers—
so he asked for your last name, but I couldn't remember
no matter how hard I tried.
Going down the list in my mind,
yours was the only one—a blank space
where my heart and mind,
maybe soul,
used to be.
No surprise.
It's been fifteen years.
Why would I? Why should I?
You left me months before I walked out the door.
I was too much.
You weren't enough—*at least that's what you told yourself.*
Nothing would change your mind.
You wouldn't let it, and, now, you are gone.
So, here we are, again, after all this time.
Me,
trying to feel.
You,
resurrected—
a nameless shadow on the tip of my tongue
that escapes me, as always.
My friend thought it sad to have been dead for so long
without anyone noticing,
but that is the way you wanted it.
Damn your love
of needles and straws and backroom shame!
Damn, you
and your enemies within,
for not believing you were worth more!
No, you won't get my tears—not this time.
You've had your fill.
Bet they still taste as sweet.
But, you can have my hate, dear Joshua.
Neither of us needs it,
anymore.

life in/verse

thoughts flow through the air
like drifts of grey ash from a burning tower,
scorching across white sheets
like cigarette burns.

to some, words sound foreign and strange—
no rhyme or reason—
but not to those who listen
in tongues.

for sooth
of my Muse's vanity,
compulsion rules.
mad scribblings abound.

i disturb the peace of blank pages
with the moving pictures of my silent film,
fettering time
before it dissolves like sugar in the rain.

Burn

Life is slow
here in a border town,
where lazy palms
scantly twitch in dead breezes—
dry and pollen-choked.
Everywhere.
Nowhere.
Cattle,
brown against my hand
and an expanse of cloudless blue,
meander aimlessly,
chewing cud
that never quite hits the spot.
Their eyes, like minds—
blank—
closed to things made new
by the blessing of the sun,
cast downward
upon cracks and clods of grey clay
underfoot,
where a fire burns beneath the ground.
Life is slow
here in a border town,
where—in-kind—
like a shadow
I wait for a shift,
the balm of a breeze
to kiss the delicate yellow from the retama
and pave my road.
Everywhere.
Nowhere.
Noon rages overhead
(Devil's at the crossroads)
as flames whip and lick the sky,

beckoning
just beyond the watery promise
of the horizon.
So, I close my eyes
here in this border town—
everywhere,
nowhere—
seeing white
and the blood
that courses through my veins,
dig my toes into the ground, and slowly
burn.

Digging for Lost Temples

Thumbing through *The Borderlands*, I can't help but feel not "brown" enough. I'm Mexican Lite. Got a case of the "coconuts". There are no rageful battle-cries inflaming this breast. No bitterness lingering on the tip of the tongue (the back of hands and the starch of white collars taste just the same no matter the bearer's color). No tortured soul, longing for identity and re-appropriation. Just me and this suit of rosy-beige meat that touts my value best in the dead of winter.

"If you're not pissed, you aren't paying attention," some people say. Others, "We're nothing but second-class citizens—wetbacks—to them!" (My back dried three generations ago!) Then, there's all this talk of The Wall, as if one had actually never existed before in the first place. How funny people are when the invisible begin to reflect the Spectrum of Things in the cruel clarity of daylight— ancient atrocities shining, unforgivingly, like newly minted coins under brusque fluorescents. When did symbols become more real than the things they represented? (Maybe around the same time 'detention centers' and 'concentration camps' meant different things?) "Better them than me," I would think to myself. "Everyone's got to hate someone, right?"

Call it apathy. Detachment. Indifference. Call it what you like, but don't let an absence of tears convey a treason of the flesh. I know where I come from and where my people have been. I am one of the many brown bodies that was piled in heaps, used as target practice by Texas Rangers that stood proudly before them, posing for photographs. I swung low from sturdy boughs in the Southwest, proving Strange Fruit—plucked in all its hues and flavors—tastes coppery and bitter in Life's maw. I starved outside with the rest of the dogs, staring into diner windows—mind, body, and spirit consumed—barred from entry, wanting for crumbs. The narrative's my own, but the story remains the same.

I'm no one's *machisto*, gangbanger, Latin lover, wetback, or Spic. I am no one's pimp, *Sancho, caballero,* or *maricon*. I can't roll my Rs, I hate tequila, and I don't code switch. Sheepskins—paid by my own coin—adorn my walls, not holographic portraits of "The Last Supper" or La Santa Muerte adorned with plastic red roses from the dollar store. I am not "spicy" like something that is novelly consumed. And I—a being, self-determined, not cast from a vulgar mold— respect God's will as much as he respects mine (which doesn't say much).

The blood of peasants and slaves, warriors and kings run through our veins. Our ears once heard gods' whispers through the rustling of leaves in the breeze and the trickling of streams over time-smoothed stones. We rode the winds—the sun kissing our backs (not breaking them)—as we flew through fields of pale azure upon Serpent's wings, over treetops and verdant expanses. We ate our enemies' courage and drank victor's wine with lips, stained red, from their skulls. (So, step back with your 'tallboys' and that Four Lokos jive!) This is what lies beneath the skin. Melanin be damned! We are the sons and daughters of Earth and Sky, Aztec Temples of Sun and Moon, buried beneath blanched soil, crowned by cathedrals—papal tiaras anointed by brown blood that pepper the land like so many gravestones.
Remember?
Remember!

So, I pray to the Archangel Anzaldua to help me find my lost sovereignty—my words wafting up into the clouds on velvety ropes smoke of sandalwood incense and braided sweetgrass. Tears of honey fall from Heaven upon my skin, feeding cuts and scrapes no one (not even I) can see. Unfolding her rainbow-hued wings, like Hebe on Olympus, she descends with arms outstretched and an angelic smile. Face-to-face, she pulls me close, blesses my forehead with *champurrado*-scented kisses then tugs at my ear and says with the fire of cinnamon on her tongue, "*Huerco*, just love the skin you're in!"

Cajeta (Gimme Some Sweet!)

"Gimme some sweet!"
we scream
blessed by your MAD words
BAD words
GLAD words
SAD
letting them scorch palates
y quemar nuestros labios
like Holy Wafers
in the Devil's mouth.
Give us a taste
of life
your *loco*—
salty and caramel-kissed—
with every candy-flip of the page
forming crystalizations
of lithium-pink
opiate rock (candy)
on dripping tips of *lenguas*
(so ready)
that hunger for the taste
of sweet poets' milk
melting rains of cajeta
upon wanting chins and souls
under hot breaths of your WICKED verse.

"Gimme some sweet!"
gritamos
longing for a fix—
ecstatic
spasmatic
orgasms—
of your word-sugar
(tus palabras dulces)

their velvety, fatal stabs
to the heart
(mi corazón)
and the backs of throats
(releasing bad blood and MAD words)
like glistening Astro Pops
sharpened and honed
by the spit and rolling tongues
of PrOphETS—
their anointing mouths
and bleeding pens
working their *brujería*—
confectionate necromancies—
upon lifeless eardrums
y *animas*
that languished bitterly
in reductive states
of silent subtraction.

C'mon…

Gimme some sweet!
(Some candied teats to suckle)
Gimme some sweet!
(Sticky trickles of sanctified honey-nectar)
Gimme some sweet!
(El fuego…la alma en mi sangre)
Gimme some sweet!
(Good, proper skull-fucks that inject your Truths)
Gimme some sweet!
(A case of "the sugars" that never felt so good)
Ándale! Dame tu dulce
y no me dejais aquí estropeado!
(Don't leave me here CRASHING)

Coda-Switch

O, viejas de negro!
How you line the front pews
at Catholic masses
like pushers sitting on street curbs,
rolling rosary beads—
like pills of black-tar heroin—
between jonesing fingers,
craving elusive fixes of salvation,
visiones de Dios.
Such beastly things
behind those lifeless veils of pitch!
Those guttural mumbles
under *respiraciones y lenguas,*
drunk with righteousness,
acrid and rank
with the smell of death
and the sour of Communal wine.
Spells of atonement, maybe?
Curses of chastity?
Oraciones por mi?
Oh, I think not! *(Creo que no!)*

Why shouldn't our ecstasies—
in all their corporal glory—compare?
Aren't Heaven's truths just as easily scried
amongst kaleidoscopes
of gas-streaked street puddles…
…the glorious freckles of smooth, bare backs and shoulders…
the shapes left behind in dampened sheets the morning after?
O, divine geomancies!
How I love
(need)
our alchemy—the transmutations
of magnificent bodies of light
and living streams that shimmer hot and wet,

setting skin and lips
(nuestra piel y labios)
aflame.
All that is good is gold,
but nothing gold can stay*
for even the most treasured of God's sparrows
fall from flight,
silently screaming,
impaling
upon the holy stabs of His Electric Crown of Thorns.
So, let's dwell on patches of fragrant grasses
and sip (not sin) from our gardens' springs
O, sacred elixir!
partaking of flesh and blood—
our Eucharist—
devouring, 'til all is gone,
shining, *brillante*,
against shadows of cold piety
cast by dark, ringless Brides of the Lord,
before the hues of the day bleed away
into pale shades that
powder and crumble to dust
under the gravity of God's thumb (love). Amen.

*Line taken from Robert Frost's "Nothing Gold Can Stay" (1923)

little deaths

We implode—
explode—
in raptures
of liquid light
that set the skin
to sizzle on the spit
like slow-cooked meat,
pulled apart
in greedy clutches,
peeling
skin from skin,
limb from limb,
sinew from bone
until all is gone,
fallen away
in shreds
and trickles.
Tongues prodding,
hungrily,
for the taste of coppery bliss
of chewed lips.
Beautiful bodies—
diminished
into heartbeats and exhales
of viscera and vasculature
with eyelids, aflutter—
fade
into black, into white,
into black, again—
dick-teasing,
mind-fucking
strobes of abstract consciousness.

Hand-in-hand,
together,
we die
little deaths,
again…
again…
and again—
every morning, a resurrection.

Duende

Green is the taste of bitter rind that lingers on your fingertips,
cutting through the sweetness of icebox orange smiles
bursting on my tongue, lovingly fed,
conjuring the salty sting of solitude's imminence,
as if a shade.

How dreaded the tic-toc of the clock—
rhythmic shower of dying heartbeats—
hanging, sourly, above us in white clusters,
promising much, offering little
but that which is within our fleshy grasps.
Before dawn breaks and you slip away—a shadow
fleeing the Eye of Day—
you reach backward, hand upon wanting hip, pulling me inward,
stopping time if but for a second longer.

O morning thief!
I am bound by your fragrant tethers
that permeate, infiltrate 'the everything' under my skin
through the hole in my chest that once held a beating heart,
long-since cast at the pink of your delicate arches.
My soul quivers as you turn and smile,
then walk away,
leaving behind your indentions and a tattered Lorca,
tossed afloat in the rising, orange currents of morning.

Still, I am drawn to the darkness of my corners,
where Death has found a home.
The purity of her black light defines, reveals all
within this drowned world of light and shadow.
There is no love without fear of absence,
no hope without doubt,
no fulfillment without the memory of Hunger's dull stabs.
We savor and rejoice these fleeting moments—
all that is good under God's blue heaven—
for in the end
all we are left with…all that is true…
is that cold taste of green.

Eating Pears on the Rooftop

Come!
Let us eat pears—
green and cold—
at night on the rooftop
under burdened boughs of the old yew
and the moon's pale glow.
Let us love
and laugh
at myths and shadow-plays
born of sticks and stones and celestial light—
the stuff of illusion
(delusion)
that pulls us far from the cold comfort
of home.
There, the close confines of our rooms lie, prepared,
untouched by the deceits of night and day—
welcoming and pure.
O, to be with you in the dark
(boundlessness within those walls)
behind thick curtains of rich brown and verdant green—
that glorious place of undiscerning Truth,
where glamours crumble to dust
(to dust).
To this
we say, "Yes! Yes! Yes!"
and kiss the silver from each other's lips—
sticky and sweet—
each soft brush
a rap on the front door.

www.ingramcontent.com/pod-product-compliance
Lightning Source LLC
LaVergne TN
LVHW041511070426
835507LV00012B/1493